"I like poetry that asks big questions yet showers us with elements of security. I find that central theme in James D. Frisbie's *Skeptical Believer* to be essential to the core of life and faith itself. That alone makes it a notable read for anyone."

—John Nilsen, Professional Musician

"As friends and pastors, Jim and his wife Rinya have been integral in my faith journey. Like their wise counsel, the *Skeptical Believer* looks at all sides of spiritual questioning. Jim's tight, evocative imagery brings comfort to all who walk the convoluted road of faith versus doubt."

—Dixie Siegel, Retired English teacher

"This beautiful collection of poetry offers moments for introspection, questions for reflection, words or phrases that give one pause, and poignant insights that break or delight one's heart; words to be savored."

—Barbara Nixon, Coordinator, Interfaith Voices column

"Every person of faith will relate to this beautiful book of free verse poetry. We all have had occasional, sometimes sustained, bouts of skepticism, cynicism, doubt, fear, or spiritual emptiness. Yet, within all of us is a deep-seated desire, as James D. Frisbie affirms in his concluding poem, 'to live a life where every moment matters.' *Skeptical Believer's* honest wrestling with questions of life and faith will reawaken within you God's holy imagination and fill you once again with wonder, love, and praise."

—Bruce R. Ough, Retired Bishop, The United Methodist Church

"Many people struggle with situations in life that arise from spiritual questioning—sometimes due to personal crises or conflicts, sometimes triggered by the turpitude of the world. But spiritual searching also comes rooted in the daily ordinariness of life, sometimes in the wonder of creation, and sometimes in profound spiritual moments when we experience the presence of the Divine; our soulful musings can move us to a deeper faith. In *Skeptical Believer*, author,

theologian, and poet James D. Frisbie offers his musings to touch our hearts and deepen our spiritual journeys. This collection of poems offers the reader an open door leading to one's own reflection and spiritual journey."

—Robert T. Hoshibata, Retired Bishop,
The United Methodist Church

Skeptical Believer

Skeptical Believer

Thoughts and Questions on Life and Faith

Written by JAMES D. FRISBIE

Foreword by *Charles R. Ault Jr.*

Photos by *Rinya L. Frisbie*

RESOURCE *Publications* • Eugene, Oregon

SKEPTICAL BELIEVER
Thoughts and Questions on Life and Faith

Resource Publications
An Imprint of Wipf and Stock Publishers
199 W. 8th Ave., Suite 3
Eugene, OR 97401

www.wipfandstock.com

PAPERBACK ISBN: 979-8-3852-6911-2
HARDCOVER ISBN: 979-8-3852-6912-9
EBOOK ISBN: 979-8-3852-6913-6

Edited by A Word's Worth, LLC.

Contents

Foreword

A Poetic Tonic for Restless Souls

To those uneasy about making a leap of faith into belief, for those who have drifted away from making religious practice central to their daily living, and for those ensconced in a materialistic world view—I recommend paying close attention to poet and pastor James D. Frisbie's *Skeptical Believer*. The author begins his metaphorical excursion into his own inner life with the provocative question, "What is real?" In place of metaphysical analysis, he pursues an answer with crisp images and sharp reflections that open his inner self to honest appraisal of the world and what his Christian heritage has taught him to believe.

Rinya Frisbie's stunning photographs—each a metaphor in and of themselves—introduce stanzas of interconnected poems. The fragmented trunk of a burnt tree snapped by the wind reflects the omnipresent fragility of life, a truth triumphant over "dogmatic security" and essential to satisfying the thirst of the soul, a truth for the church to embrace in breaking through to new ideas.

The faith revealed in the poems of *Skeptical Believer* is more stance than belief. This stance is grounded in reverence and wonder; it finds depth, meaning, and awe in the face of commonplace events. This stance honors the reality of poverty and the healing power of love.

Frisbie's poems reverberate in mind and heart, prompting the reader to pause and reflect upon the inscrutable mystery that abounds in every dimension of experience. His poetry lures the skeptic and the agnostic to reconsider and reimagine the place of the church's teachings to help a skeptical believer find faith.

—Charles "Kip" Ault
Professor Emeritus
Lewis & Clark College
Portland, Oregon, USA

Acknowledgments

THE ORIGIN OF THIS book can be traced back to the process of writing free verse during the Two Year Academy for Spiritual Formation which I participated in during 1989–1991 at the Holy Wisdom Monastery (formerly the St. Benedict Center) in Madison, Wisconsin. I am deeply grateful for the acceptance and encouragement of the participants and leaders during that time. They gave me the courage to embrace my lingering questions and allow my faith to mature as I anchored it in these poems.

I also want to acknowledge someone farther back in my life. Gwen Coumbe was an elderly friend who lived near campus during my college years, and she was the one who encouraged me to keep a journal. I was preparing for my junior year abroad at the University of Ghana, and she said, "Jim, keep a journal. Start today! If you don't, you will never do it…." I took her at her word, and it was the beginning of my literary journey.

I want to express deep appreciation to my wife and partner in ministry, Rinya, for her tolerance, support, and encouragement, as well as her photos that liven up these pages.

One last note: I want to thank my editor, Teri Watanabe of A Word's Worth, LLC, for her expertise and help in turning my rough ramblings into carefully crafted poems.

No good thing is ever the work of only one person, and I hope this book communicates the formative impact that so many have had on my life.

Introduction

HAVE YOU EVER ASKED, "What is real?" Have deep and troubling questions emerged in your spiritual life?

As I came to grips with my own discomfort with the religious traditions and doctrines that formed my faith, I began to give more credence to the questions and doubts that presented themselves. Many of the spiritual teachers and mentors who touched my life over the years were non-conformists who challenged the traditional thinking of "religion" with their questions and logic. I found that I was not alone in my skepticism. I found a path to faith through my questions. I discovered and embraced profound mystery. I felt small in the shadow of an expanding universe and yet empowered by the wonder of it all.

During the two-year course of an Academy for Spiritual Formation, I began to form the free-verse poems that comprise the heart of this collection. At first I was hesitant to share my rambling thoughts, but my fellow academy members were a receptive and supportive audience. They are the ones who encouraged me to find the courage to publish. I still hear one reader's emphatic words, "Jim, you have to publish this!"

I have come to see this form of writing as a visual art. I paint pictures, images, and scenarios with words and phrases. I want you to see in your own mind what I am describing, put yourself in that setting, and connect the cameo to the big picture of all of life in its mysterious wonder.

1

What Is Real?

Hungry for a Metaphor

I need a metaphor
to live by,
an image or template
to gauge my journey's progress.

Am I at ease,
or cast adrift?
Do I fight the good fight
or kick against the goads?

I have so few measures
to correct my course.
There is no white line
on the Spirit's highway.

I cling to scripture
but I seldom read it.
I speak of prayer
but neglect the depth
of practicing meditation.

To be a disciple is not
the stuff of heroes
but child's play
intent upon the Kingdom.

God is not all mystery!
There are lessons in the clay
and daily wisdom
in each other's eyes.

I need a metaphor
to live by,
an image of the face of Jesus
to guide my journey's progress.

Skeptical Believer

I am a skeptical believer
testing each tradition,
looking for the logic
in doctrines and beliefs.

Some people seem so certain
of their vision of heaven and hell,
gleaning the details of eternity
from snatches of scripture.

I am not so certain.
I look askance at such prophets,
quietly dismissing
their self-aggrandizing polemics.

I can't help engaging
the logic I have learned,
measuring credibility
by what I know to be true.

The mysteries of the cosmos
are too vast to be contained
in the pages of some book
conceived by ancient minds.

I seek the answers
to the unasked questions.
I ponder the unseen
and reach into the unknown.

I have few guides for this.
No one knows this part of the forest,
and few are willing to share this journey
to the place where light bends back upon itself.

What Is Real?

"What is 'real'?"
said the priest
to the shaman
as they walked
in the dust one day.

Silence followed.

Then the shaman replied,
"What you seek
is not the truth
but a tune
to dance to."

The Quest

To seek a cause
worthy of a life-consuming quest
is a set of questions
not to be asked lightly.

Questions asked
tend to get answered.
Every pilgrim
soon finds a goal
for their wandering spirit.

There is no shortage
of life-consuming causes.
People are "eaten"
every day.

But to choose
or be chosen by
one that gives life,
that itself is a quest
in the making.

New Wings

What would it take
to step across that line?
To feel the mysterious impetus
of life in its raw form?

Lift depends on gravity
to weigh down the air
lest nothing fly or breathe,
an irony of the earth.

What we take for granted
are the essentials of life,
ignoring the power
within and around us.

At my age I should be wiser.
I have the degrees,
the travel, the training
and experience.

But I feel like a beginner
emerging from some
psychic cocoon
seeing the world afresh.

Can I trust
these new wings
new eyes
new everything?

Crack the Mantle

If I were
to suddenly awake
from this somnolent life,
what would I see?

Would reality
beyond perception
offer the ultimate
"Of course!"?

If I were suddenly aware
of what exists beyond the reach
of my feeble senses,
what cosmic reality would emerge?

I live in the shadow
of my own thoughts
yet I know there is so much more
beneath the skin of sense and cognition.

The mystic in me
chafes under
the self-imposed limits
of my perceptual cocoon.

Is it possible
to crack
the mantle of life
as I know it?

And, if I could,
would I risk
the irreversible change
of venturing into that wide world?

Muddlin' in the Middle

I'm no saint.
I'm not even
a very good sinner.

I'm just muddlin'
in the middle
often fearful
slow to act
and apt to miss
the golden opportunity.

It would be sad to grow old
without a few stellar moments
when my inner light
shined bright and true.

Who knows?
I still breathe
think
and feel.

My powers are not gone;
my day is not yet over.
In fact
my life may be
just beginning.

Christ Comes Running

Christ comes running,
eyes bright with joy
to shatter the ice inside me
with laughter and a hug.

"But I'm not worthy . . ."
does not cut it with such a deity.
Who am I to dampen his party
with my fumbling for humble words?

Holy parties don't happen
on my command,
only on my account
when this lavish Lord
sees an inch of growth in me.

Faith

To believe or not
that there is within me
and around me a divine presence
at work in the world

This is the challenge of faith

To believe in the hidden power,
sentient, pervasive, more real
than my own existence

I am like a fish
questioning the existence of water,
allowing doubt to alienate me
from my source and sustenance

Faith is an act of courage

To step out of the boat
in the midst of the storm,
responding to the One
who beckons me to "Come!"

Four-Part Harmony

The fourth part of the Trinity is me,
a simple unholy human
giving meaning and completion
to divinity.

Father, Son, and Holy Spirit,
holy, divine, and senseless
without the human quadrant
of existence.

My being human
allows God to be God.
Without me and all of my kind
messing up and falling on our faces
then rising to try again,
God's existence would be
empty perfection.

Suddenly creation
makes sense!
And life with God
becomes a circle dance.

Up Side Down

Loving me
is God's initial business.
Obedience
is mine.

To be still
and welcome
God's amazing warmth
is a radical move.

I cannot love God
without this
primal act
of bonding recognition.

The first commandment
of living as a human
is the willful act
of being loved.

Grace

There is an audacity about grace
that frightens me.
What would I become
if I were set free from guilt and shame?

I cannot identify the stern finger
pointing, saying, "Shame on you!"
But I know its echo by the sensation
tightening the back of my neck.

I see the residue bubbling up
like the stink from mud pots,
surprising me with my words and actions
out of line with my cherished values.

I have not survived my childhood.

Grace promises release and
welcomes dying and new birth,
a re-incarnation
of my present life.

Perhaps salvation is more real
more personal, more immanent than before,
more necessary than I had imagined—
a spiritual lifeline at my fingertips.

If grace is real at all
it must be my gift
along with the rest
of God's human family.

Coming Home

Coming home
after a year far afield
I wondered, "Will they know me?
Will I know them?"

Ten dollars in my pocket
flying stand-by
planning my
tentative re-entry.

The last flight north had a seat.
I wondered, looking down
through the dusk at familiar fields,
"How do I do this?"

I wanted to slow things down,
walk the two miles to the house,
find the hidden key, and
let myself in calling out, "I'm home!"

But as I started down
the steps of the turboprop
I saw my father standing
by the gate marked "Arrivals."

I found out later
he had met
every flight
that day.

I know now what it is
to have a father
and to be
a beloved son.

I will never fear the dark
or the coming unknown,
aware that no matter when I arrive
He will be waiting with tears in His eyes.

2

Beyond Ourselves

On the Edge

There is a town on the edge
where people dwell;
it lies south of the river
on a hill beneath fir trees.

It is a place of hope and fear
promise and wonder
where a little girl
catches a snowflake on her tongue
because she has never seen one before.

This town is suspect of strangers,
full enough of those well known
to glance sidelong
at any newcomer.

It is Bethlehem in the twenty-first century,
oblivious to its perfection,
blind to its blessing,
a hidden miracle within its walls.

Who will shine a star
on the birth about to be?
Are there no wise men ready
to walk across the street?

God is at work here
crying in a cradle,
calling to the people
who dwell on the edge.

There Is a Pastor Who Walks

There is a pastor who walks
to his church each Sunday.
In fact, he walks to five churches
on a circuit of thirty miles.

He is a circuit rider without the ride,
a prophet in sandals and sweat
toiling for his saving God
among his hurting, hopeful people.

He prays as he walks
and sometimes sings
never lacking for something to say
when the people gather.

I drive to my church
a scant half-mile
from my comfortable home
to a modern sanctuary.

I drive because I am pressed for time
by my scattered, complex life,
and often I struggle for words of grace
for my hurting, hopeful people.

Perhaps if I walked like my African brother,
sometimes praying, or even singing,
I might find a new voice
in the echo of his footsteps.

I Want a Church

I want a church
that is more
than good preaching
and great music.

I want a church
that is more than
Bible studies
and help for the poor.

I want a church
that goes beyond
fellowship gatherings
and youth activities.

I want a church
that stretches
my understanding of God
and of who I am.

I want a church
where children
can color outside the lines
and it's OK.

I want a church
where new ideas
are embraced for their merit
not abandoned for their cost.

I want a church
that is unafraid
of what the neighbors
might think.

I want a church
where funerals
are seen as
new beginnings.

I want a church
where weddings
are not just for
the bride and her mother.

I want a church
that gives more than it takes
and fits into the landscape
like an old, old tree.

I want a church
of possibilities,
new images
and vision.

I want a church
where God comes often
and lingers long
in the hearts of the people.

I want a church
where no one is at fault
and forgiveness
happens.

I want a church
unafraid of failure,
afloat on
God's grace.

I want a church
where God is in charge
as each one yearns to catch
a vision of the divine design.

I want a church,
not so much to attend
as to carry into the world
like a laptop or smartphone.

I want a church
that lives in me
and, because it does,
I touch the hand of God.

Eucharist

Eucharist is soul feeding,
many faces, hands, and hearts
breaking the bread,
holding the cup,
blessing each other eye to eye.

In the broken bread
I hold the broken world in my hands.
The cup of blessing lifts my downcast face,
and in the blending of sorrow and joy
it flavors and deepens my life.

I cannot be whole
without being broken bread.
I cannot see God
unless I drink deep.

In these symbols of reality
my life takes on significance,
compassion, unity,
and power.

Eucharist is soul feeding,
many faces, hands, and hearts,
sharing the bread and the cup,
blessing each other eye to eye.

When People Pray

What happens
when people pray?
Not much
at first
on the outside.

But when
the Spirit comes
and the vision
takes hold
an engaging fire is born.

Why pray
when there is work
to be done?
Why linger
with much to do?

Our best efforts
turn to dust
and our passion
drifts like blown sand
when there is no center.

What happens
when people pray?
God comes,
and the past is lost
in present glory.

What happens
when people pray?
Healing comes,
convictions change,
like a pear ripening
from the inside out.

What happens
when people pray?
Not much
at first
on the outside . . . .

There Is a Future

Doing good is worth the effort,
not today
but down the road it builds
a bank account of character.

Oh, the generous and loving deeds
so often seem to flow
outward and away like water
poured onto the ground.

But the earth never
forgets a kindness
and life has its ways.

If I had a choice,
and I do,
I would choose to side
with the grass and the flowers.

Doing good
is worth the effort,
not today
but down the road.

The One I Met

I met a lesbian today
walking by a cold stone church.
She didn't seem that different
from other women I have known.

"I went inside there once," she said.
"The people seemed to know
and looked at me with furtive glances.
I overheard someone say,
'What's she doing here?'
The pastor seemed hesitant
to shake my hand.
I doubt the choir would welcome
my alto voice."

She told me she was a healer
well respected on the job
trusted by her neighbors
to feed their cats and collect their mail
when they are away.

She is greeted at the bank
with a smile
and at the dry cleaners
by her first name.

She and her partner
own a home
pay their taxes
and go dancing on the weekends.

She reads her Bible
prays each day
and longs for a community of believers
to share her heart and spiritual journey.

I told her
of my church
and breathed a prayer
of hope.

Would we, could we
accept this seeking soul
with open minds,
open hearts, open doors?

Would there be a place
in our choir for her alto voice,
a place among the seekers
for her questions and her tears?

I met a woman today
not unlike others
I have known
but with a uniqueness
born of God
to challenge my perspective.

Perhaps her presence
tells my tale more than hers—
the challenge and the questions
stretching my mind and heart
to understand the many mysteries
of God's good creation.

It Is the Poor

It is the poor
who know
what it is
to be crucified

Money is armor
property a fortress
status employs the law
on its own behalf

It is the poor
who are called
"lazy . . . loser . . . welfare queen"
though they work two jobs

It is the poor
who are clubbed and cuffed
before any questions
are asked

It is the poor
who are judged by color
despised for what they wear
and fed cast-off garbage

It is the poor
who know what it is to be crucified
Perhaps that is why Jesus
loves them more than you and me

3

Breaking Through

Through

The way through
is to go through
despair to hope
sorrow to joy
loneliness to desire
death to life
fear to peace

In the going
there is dying
Who am I not
to be afraid?

Yet I know
no other passage
I have no other moment
than the now

The way through
is to go through

The Middle Way

The middle way is hard.
I step gingerly between
Pharisees witch-hunting for sin
and Sadducees who deny
the power of the resurrection.

Sometimes this middle way
narrows to a razor blade
slicing my feet
with every step.

But then again
sometimes it is
a mountain meadow path
pulsing with new life.

I will walk this middle way
because my thirst for truth
is greater than my need
for dogmatic security.

Being in touch
with what is real
brings more satisfaction
than dozens of frightened followers.

By His Wounds

How did you know
so long ago and far away
that I would need such grace?

I thought I was doing fine
till my straight-ahead gaze
was seeing nothing but sky

How did you know???

Oh, I dance and laugh
so much of the time
ignoring the finer points of sin

I ride on pride or swim in self-pity
till words from the Word
lay bare my festering need

How did you know
so long ago and far away
that I would need such grace?

Courage

It's the courage part
of faith
which gives me
the most trouble.

It's not easy being brave
when mystery
is the better part
of believing.

I tremble
when challenged.
I cannot help myself.
Love has no "heart" in me.

I wilt under fire.
I bend with the wind.
I hide from the thunder
and run from the rain.

Yet in my quiet moments
I choose the way of love
and ground myself again
in the One who knows no fear.

Mercy

When I feel doubt
mercy shines through
the cracks
in my doubts and fears

When I feel despair
mercy brings joy
where I least
expect it

When all seems lost
mercy shows me
the golden key
hiding in my pocket

Mercy is the power
of God's lavish abundance
made real
in human experience

Mercy teaches me once again
that God is real
and life is good
beyond my wildest expectations

Do You Love Me?

Do you love me?
Is it a question
or an accusation?

It matters
who is asking—
Tevia, Jesus,
a spouse, a child.

There is a haunting quality
to the question,
suspicious of betrayal,
longing for affirmation.

"Do you love me?"
is the existential query
delving to the heart
of what it means to be human.

To be loved, or not,
fills my cup or drains it,
determining my trajectory
to heaven or to hell.

Baptized

Baptized,
bought with a price,
Christ invested in me
at my naming.

Grace is fluid
like water,
splashing and laughing
like a mountain stream
unconcerned about
the persistence of its source.

Only a lavish God
would baptize a baby
long before that child
could rise to any standard
of worth or expectation.

I was baptized
simply because I was loved.
Anything more that day
was just harmony
to God's melody.

Gratitude

Gratitude moves me to feel
and to give
and to love the one
who loves me most.

My blessings
have limits.
My doubts and fears
constrain my generosity.

But God,
the unseen giver
urges my heart to see
a vision not my own.

Who am I
to squeeze the life
from God's
fragile gifts?

To breathe freely
in this life
I must breathe
in *and* out.

To know blessings
and grace
means to both
accept and give.

Gratitude moves me
when I need it most
as giving and receiving
express the breath of life.

Morning Eucharist

A Shoshoni friend taught me
to rise each day drink water and say,
"Thank you, for another day of living."

To live each day as a gift of God
is my primordial eucharist
sharing my blood and flesh with all creation.

4

The Light Within

The Unseen Light

There is an unseen light
that guides my way,
an unseen mystic breeze
turning my face to immortality.

It is both intimate and universal
a cosmic presence
like gravity.
A Jedi would know it.

It is so subtle I can easily lose it.
Following the unseen light
takes all my attention
like flying the glideslope
of an instrument approach.

I have come to trust
this unseen light
yet my focus wanders
and I stumble.

Though my attention wavers
the light does not.
It remains true,
waiting for my reconnection to
and reception of its truth.

Am I mad or foolish
to trust such an ethereal guide?
Or is it truly a portal
to the meaning of life?

The Power of Beauty

Beauty has the power
to make us good.
Wonder inspires
a passion for the Holy.

We discover our inner
virtue of generosity
when awe
puts us in our place.

I saw the power of beauty
in a hummingbird
spent and frantic
on the inside of a window,
gently captured
and set free by a boy
with sky blue eyes.

We are rich or poor
not by the measure of our money
but by our awareness of wonder
lifts our hearts to glory.

Healing Hands

Who has felt
the healing hands of Jesus?
Who has known
the wonder of His touch?

What kind of God is this
who dares to reach across the void
to shed the distance of deity
for the sake of a wounded soul?

Jesus walks among us,
fully aware of his threatening presence,
unconcerned with our reluctance;
compassion alive in His eyes.

In the mystery of healing touch
hope is born.
Our soul-wounds are not mortal
unless we make them so.

Who has felt
the healing hands of Jesus?
Who has known
the wonder of his touch?

God's Dream

What power
does a dream have
to shape
a life of faith?

Who can see
beyond the curved horizon
to the other side
of possibility?

Where are we
when God gets creative?
Are we sleeping
or just busy?

God's dream
makes love possible.
God's dream is hope
with sacred wounds.

God's dream
is the salvation
of the world
one child at a time.

We are living
in God's dream,
complete with color,
sound and light.

What power
does a dream have
to shape
our life of faith?

Still

When I am still
my soul catches up with me.
It's an old African proverb
true in my experience.

It is not always comfortable.
Regrets, embarrassment
and lost opportunity tumble
helter-skelter into the present.

My task in stillness
is to sort them out,
savor my successes,
shake out the chaff.

My days travel
at the speed of life
leaving few opportunities
for the luxury of sacred stillness.

I seek the solitary place within
to culture and cultivate
the inner light and compass
that renews my sense of who I am.

Love Is Not the Stranger

Love is not the stranger
that I thought she was
but closer now
and with a subtle warmth

I feel the power of God
around me and within
in ways that challenge
change and verify

No, love is not the stranger
that I thought she was

Love Centers Me

Love centers me,
cutting through
the worry
of a busy life
ill-spent
on many tangents.

I chase
after things
on the edges
of meaning,
frothy goals
of passing interest.

But love centers me,
drawing me back
with a snap
to what is real,
deep,
lasting.

I cease to be owned by issues
others deem important,
captive to
hype,
fads,
and pressure
to conform.

Love is my genesis,
and my destination,
lived in real life and
centered
in the paradox
of God.

Love Changes

Love changes.
The circle widens and deepens
from passion to pathos
like a hug interrupted
by little arms and legs
wanting to be a part of it.

Love changes
when touch becomes softer
with time and repetition,
a note of healing
where once was exploration,
like the last sip of wine
is different from the first.

Love changes
to where an argument
can take us deeper into mystery
than making love,
and the passing of time opens doors
we pass through together
rather than alone.

Love changes
from courtship to altar,
birthing room to office,
challenging growing up
with growing down,
intimacy with self-disclosure,
life together with dying to be reborn.

5

Times & Seasons

This Is a Time

This is a time for seekers and dreamers
to look up and catch a snowflake
like a spacecraft from another world
marveling at the unique array of feathery crystals.

This is a time for seekers and dreamers
to wonder what lies behind
the eyes of those
who hurry past.

This is a time for seekers and dreamers
to peer into a cold clear sky
and try to feel the magnitude
of the stellar lights.

This is a time for seekers and dreamers
to look for ways to make a difference
itching for significance
hungry for heart-food.

This is a time for seekers and dreamers
to be angry at the mystery,
confounded by the paradoxes
essential to God's creation.

This is a time for seekers and dreamers
to look for the baby in a manger,
convinced of the power of love,
and find their answers in the stillness of the night.

Christmas Rainbow

Christmas is full of surprises,
like a sudden rainbow
against a dark sky.

The faces of Christmas
are no less surprising:
the cheerful mail carrier,
the pharmacist in the silly hat,
the five-year-old catching
a snowflake on her tongue.

God is made real
in each manger scene,
and the eyes of Jesus twinkle
behind every Santa's beard.

Hope

Hope sees
around corners
and over the curvature
of the earth.

Hope moves like a baby
in the womb
and dances like a snowflake
through the trees.

Hope whispers
the impossible
and makes believers
of the most ardent skeptics.

Hope guides the Magi
inside our hearts
and makes us wonder
about the most ordinary star.

Hope flickers
like a candle
and shines brightly
in the dim light of midnight.

Hope brings us to life
and back again,
remembering our origin
in the hands of a loving God.

The Babe of December

What good
is a newborn baby?
Is it the object of our love
and expectation?

What benefit comes
with his crying in the night?
What glory shows
in his neediness?

This babe, like any other
brings out the best in us,
a reaction of love
arising like a primordial urge.

God's first test
of our worthiness
comes with a cry
in the night.

Will we respond,
will we care,
will we find glory
amid the straw?

God is at work
in the babes of December
testing the softness of our metal,
opening our frozen hearts to wonder.

No Promises

I don't often make
New Year's resolutions
but I resolve
to guide
the changes
changing me.

I choose to critically assess
the forces forming
my emerging character
to decide
at least the "Who"
that guides my becoming.

I have far less control
than once I thought
to set new habits
in their place.

But I can
and will
determine deep within
the voices which
I answer to and heed.

Lord, guide these new directions
in the turning tide of time
that I may find my focus
and take a step
or two
in your direction.

Resolution

I desire to receive
willingly and joyfully
a humane heart—
the heart of Christ

To care, to risk, to love
as if there were no tomorrow
no further opportunity
no greater challenge
or higher calling

To dance life
as if no one was watching
except perhaps
the One who matters most

Day of Blessing

Valentine's is just
a day like any other,
a time to remember I am loved
and to act upon the thought.

I am blessed
by those who love me
without assessment,
judgment,
or condition.

I see in their eyes
the heart of what I can become,
my soul valued
for my inherent
worth.

It is a pity I love so little
and show it even less.
What caution robs me
of a smile, hug,
or kiss?

God is lavish
with the good things,
bringing into my life
a word of blessing
on this winter day.

Lent

Lent moves me
down into the deep
where demons lie
beside the pool.

I hesitate,
knowing the effect of the plunge.
No tether or safety line
assures the way back.

If I turn from the edge
it is a death of a different sort,
the coward's way
that never knows the other side.

Ticking time compels me.
Though I hesitate,
the way forward is clear,
dark, foreboding, and rich.

If Stones Could Talk

If stones could talk
the garden tomb
would have a tale to tell
of God's great earthquake
rattling human history.

Who could have guessed
that an unexpected tremor
would raise hopes like ripples
from an earth-borne epicenter?

We are descendants of that day
bearing the marks of resurrection.
The hope of heaven flavors all we do.
We hold life sacred, yet with a gentle touch.

That silent sermon cast in stone
has liberated our future.
We are free to rise and fall,
to live, to die, and live again.

If stones could talk
the garden tomb
would have a tale to tell
of God's great earthquake
rattling human history
and the way we see ourselves.

Being a Mother

Being a mother is tough—
bearing a child,
watching that child grow,
wondering what the child will become.

It breaks a mother's heart
to see them leave—
off to war,
away to school,
chasing dreams
of hope for far-away happiness.

I am not a mother
but I can watch.
I see pain, pride,
and anxious fear—
all in a mother's eyes.

I love my children,
but it is not the same.
To bear and birth,
cradle and nurture,
hold and set free
the young of one's heart
is a privilege and joy
reserved for women.

I am not a mother
but I have one.
I cannot be a mother
but I am married to one.
I can love her
but still, I stand
in awe of the mystery
of a mother and child.

The Summer Wind

The summer wind of God
is full of surprises,
tongues of flame
and many voices

There is an open feeling
to God's surprising spirit
that lends itself to wonder
and no small sense of fear

The life of God
in the here and now
shakes my doctrines
and easy assumptions

Who is this One
who moves so freely
with so little regard
for my expectations?

New life is born
of struggle
and comes
without a commentary

The summer wind of God
is moving the trees overhead
bringing the unseen truth
to dance across my face

Fall Skies

Fall skies are like a child's face
full of mischief and meaning
suddenly surprising
Maybe I just
have not
been looking
up

These past weeks
have been a time
of color blindness
and tunnel vision
like looking down
a paper tube
at one problem
then another

This morning's clouds
woke me up
with grey and silver
and a dozen shades of blue

I wanted to go play with them
in someone's borrowed biplane
to feel the misty beauty
on my grinning face

But for now
jogging through the sagebrush
just to see the sky again
is more than enough

It's Time

It's time to bring the harvest home—
taking stock of what I have,
settling in for the cold months
to come.

It's a busy time
cleaning and gleaning,
sorting what to keep
and what to give to the earth.

It's time, in the shortening days
to busy my heart
sorting what to store
and what to give away.

What I keep
becomes a part of me
like fruit preserved
in Mason jars.

What I give
defines my values,
showing the world
the size of my heart.

I cannot keep it all, even if I wished.
Life needs to scatter seeds,
giving back more than it takes
with an eye to next year.

I see a message
in falling leaves and cool earth.
Wisdom bids me
listen and respond.

6

Embracing Mystery

I Have Never Been This Way Before

When my spirit goes where I've never been before
I need a guide, a friend, a mentor
who knows the way
and has survived the rapids and the calm.

I need more than a vision,
more than Spirit, wind, or intuition.
I need a flesh-and-blood-real-live-servant-of-God,
not to hold my hand
but to save my bacon and my soul
from those on the exciting edges of the faith
who would see me as an edible disciple.

I need such a one.
For I have never been this way before
and two thousand years of mistakes
need not all be repeated in me.

Wind, Rain, and Fire

Our God is a God
of wind, rain, and fire—
tears, laughter, and passion
lived at the heart of life itself.

I find myself stymied
by limits and boundaries,
gothic images
of sweetness and reprimand.

"God is not like that!"
I scream or beg, "Please . . . ."
I cannot survive
a suffocating God!

If that be God's nature
I would revel
in the distance
between us.

Yet deep within,
somewhere unknown
a voice like a whisper
says my searching is shared
by the man on the cross.

God is not like
the published image.
All distance is psychic.
God's wind, rain, and fire
will someday be known,
and life with desire
will come into its own.

To Die Well

We all must die,
but some die well
with the imminent prospect
of being reborn.

The Easter experience
was meant
as a template
for faithful living.

Dying can be so deadly
as to take the life out of living,
killing hope unborn
and joy like an unwitting sacrifice.

Yet there is healing in the cross,
sunlight in the tomb
and no lack of joy in grieving
for significant losses.

O death,
where is your sting
in the midst of life
rebounding?

To die well
we must live with fire, not ice,
feeling each heartbeat
as its own miracle.

To die well
we must live in the tension
between earth and sky,
accepting the horizon
as a mirage
of our own making.

To die is our fate,
To die well
is our opportunity
and an opening door.

The Giver

We can't
out-give the Giver
who gives
from the heart.

Life is lavish.
Summer sun
and winter snows
fulfill more than just our needs.

How foolish it is to worry,
turning our baggage into burdens
when we can simply welcome
the gift with unencumbered grace.

The risk in receiving
is to become a giver too,
conforming to the image
of the One who is the source.

We can't out-give
the Giver
who gives
from the heart.

Essence of Heaven

To strive, to know,
and to be known,
to touch and to be touched—
that is the essence of heaven begun on earth.

Like the wonder
of rocking a newborn,
amazed at the distance
yet bonding in some mysterious way.

God is too much
flesh and blood!
Too real
and far too close!

We hide in doctrines
and righteous indignation,
fearful of the living truth
among us.

Knowing God is easier
than I had thought,
like longing for sleep
and letting it happen.

My search is over
and just begun,
a paradox,
like the distance
between my mind
and the babe in my arms.

Sophia

Sophia, wisdom,
the feminine image of God.
In my encounter with her
my world expands.
No longer am I the fearful child
or the predator.

For I have gazed into her eyes and kissed her.

Now I see the divine image
in feminine form as well
as masculine strength.
Now all humanity
bears the inner print of God to me
and fear gives way to wonder.

Our God

Our God is not a God
of passiveness and calm
like a craftsman sitting
quietly at a bench creating tiny tools.

No, our God is one
who feels the power of emotion,
splashing buckets of color
on the canvas of the earth.

Our God is like Zorba the Greek,
feeling joy and sorrow,
pain and ecstasy.

Our God lives in the earthquake
the fire and the storm at sea.
Our God explodes the sky
with full circle sunsets
lasting a moment
then fading to black.

Our God fills the earth with life
to the depths of the sea
and the heights
of rocky peaks.

Our God dances creation,
singing into existence
the cry of the loon
and the whisper of the white pine,
creating with a flourish and a shout
the timber wolf and the sandhill crane.

Our God
is not passive and calm
letting things be
with a ho-hum sigh.

I am lucky,
for without the image
of God in me,
what reason would I have to dance?

Life Isn't Fair

Life is seldom fair.
We reap what we sow,
but never
in the same proportion.

Life is seldom fair.
Just look at the cross,
the symbol of cruelty
and legalized injustice.

Humanity is seldom humane.
We kill our best critics
and crucify our benefactors
on trees of righteous indignation.

Yet in the divine imbalance
we live on the better half,
lucky or blessed
to get the good we don't deserve.

Life is seldom fair.
If it were
we would be doomed
to a graceless life of tit-for-tat.

Life is seldom fair.
We live in the shadow
of rainbows
and empty tombs.

On this side of glory
we dare not complain,
lest we suffer the pangs
of a well-deserved fate.

Forever

Nothing is forever—
not the earth, the sky,
the sun or the heartfelt
promises of lovers.

The word "forever"
has the sound
of foolish permanence,
a lofty wish in empty air.

I hesitate to promise forever,
turning instead to a persistent
succession of "nows," embracing
a tenacious loop of commitment.

If forever were real,
I would reject its appeal,
opting instead
for a grasp of reality.

Each day is a gift,
each sunrise a blessing,
each moment on the face of this earth
a miracle in the making.

I long to trade "forever"
for a simple "yes" to life
embracing what is and what is becoming
with childlike wonder.

7

From the Pages of Scripture

The Psalms

The Psalms
are glutinous
words and Word
binding earth and heaven.

They embody
mind-soul and creature-body
defending us from a rending dualism
and melding our theology into theophany.

Reflections on Psalm 90

God of the dinosaur,
God of amoeba,
God for whom then and now
flow into what is yet to be.

Hours and days
are our designations,
like children
waiting for recess.

Life is more
than meets the eye,
death less
than a passage.

It is God's deathless perspective
that frightens us most.
We live in the brackets
of womb and tomb.

But God calls us to see
beyond the visible spectrum of time
and to hear beyond the audible range
of our pseudo-deafness.

Teach us to count in multiples of infinity,
living by moments and lifetimes,
awed by the timeless,
moved by the momentary flicker of color.

Number our days . . .
Number our days . . .
Teach us
to number our days.

Who's in Charge???

What Jesus really said
to Nicodemus was,
"Who's in charge here?"

He said it again to Peter at Joppa
and Paul on the way to Damascus,
"Who's in charge of your life?"

I answer that question
by looking at my feet.

Admitting my own
phobic need for control
shatters it.

I know the taste of liberty
Christ-centering gives.
But oh, the task of letting go!

It is like diving off a bridge,
leaning into the air
with my helpless toes
curled around a cold steel girder.

"Who's in charge here?"

"If You Say So . . ."

(Luke 5:5)

"If you say so . . ."
is the "harrumph"
of faith
under fire.

What Simon Peter
really wanted
was to say,
"You've got to be kidding!"

All night they had worked
on the sea without success.
What does a carpenter know
about fishing?

Jesus
sometimes asks
the darndest things
of us.

We have all the practiced replies,
"It won't work."
"It never has before."
"That's not the usual way!"
Our ruts are all quite logical.

But Jesus doesn't mind
being the fool for the moment
in order to be
the hero of God's day.

Soon Peter would leave the sea
allowing this amazing carpenter
to teach him how to fish
the great wide world of humanity.

Gratitude's Gift

(Luke 17:11–17)

Ten were healed.
But nine went their way
content to celebrate
their good fortune.

One returned
to fall at the Master's feet
not willing to let the moment pass
without a word of heartfelt gratitude.

Some feel it is an imposition
if expected to say "Thank you,"
as if their pride, or sense of self,
is somehow diminished
by these simple words.

But others know the joy
that comes with meeting the Master eye to eye,
absorbing the blessing of his smile
and finding a second healing in his gaze.

Ten were healed.
Nine got lucky;
the other,
blessed.

Do You Want to Be Healed?

(John 5:1–9)

"Do you want to be healed?"
The question slices through
all denial
and self-justification.

"Do you want to be healed
of the anger and laziness
that cripple your soul?

"Do you want to be healed
so you can rejoin the pilgrims
instead of sitting
in a puddle of self-pity?

"Do you want to be healed
of past injury
that has become
a petrified idol?

"Do you want to be healed . . . ?"
Opportunities pass in a moment
and the Messiah will fade from view
all too soon.
Will you struggle to stand
at his command?
"Do you really
want to be healed?"

Dialogue

(John 4:7–15)

"Give me a drink."
"Are you sure?
Can you drink the cup
which crucifies me?"

"I am thirsty for life.
I desire an easy way,
water that has no weight
a permanent solution to my human need."

"Oh, my living water is that!
You will never
thirst again
but do you really want it?

"It is dying, you know.
Living water, thirst quenching, baptizing,
flowing-from-the-throne-of-God
living water . . . is dying.

"Can you, will you
drink from the cup that I drink?
It will satisfy your thirst,
but oh, the journey in the drinking!"

To Kick Against the Goads

As with Paul,
so am I,
doing what is wrong
with religious fervor.

The pieces of my life
do not make me whole
without divine glue
no matter how often
I place them just so.

When things fall apart,
how can I ask "Why?"
if I know it is all just me trying
to be holy, or good, or even just OK?

I'm done kicking against God's sharpened nudge.
I see the love in that encouragement
and know that gesture
of God's caring
sets me free.

Thoughts on Romans 1:16

I am not ashamed
of the Gospel
that gave my spirit birth
in farm fields and city streets.

I am not ashamed of the touch of God,
a firm hand washing my feet
or a jerk on the leash of prayer
saving me from attractive adolescent pits.

I am not ashamed
to be Bible-branded
as a preacher telling ancient tales
with stinging meanings.

I am not ashamed
to be seen by others
in the company of a rabbi
seldom honored in this world.

I am not ashamed . . . .
I am not ashamed . . . .

The Potter

The legacy of the potter
is cast in clay,
earth impervious
to decay.

The potter's work remains
as works of art or even pot sherds
ready to puzzle inquisitive
future generations.

Few of us are potters.
Our legacy is flesh and memory,
less tangible and tactile,
easily lost.

But even work
crafted in words or touch
can carry the hint of permanence
lending meaning to our moment in time.

8

For All the Saints

For All the Saints

I haven't made this journey
by myself;
there were many
who showed me the way.

There was the grizzled pastor
with a toothy grin and an old fedora
who showed me where the walleyes were
in the hole beneath the waterfall.

There was the African friend
who loved me enough
to give me his bus ticket
when weariness showed on my face.

There was the Greek woman
wise in the spirit,
a guide to the light
when I had lost my focus.

These and many others
have crossed my path
when I needed someone
to show me the way.

I would be a fool
to consider it coincidence,
ignoring the One
behind the happenstance.

I didn't make this journey
by myself.
I bow with gratitude to those
who showed me the way.

To Plant a Tree

He who plants a tree
thinks not of his own generation
but rather of the child who someday
will need to climb its leafy wonder.

I do not know how young Dad was
when first he got the urge
to bury seeds or stick a sapling
in the fertile earth.

Somewhere he learned to do it
and to wait, or go away,
trusting sun and rain and God's mystery
to do what human hands could not.

His patron saint
was Johnny Appleseed
planting trees
for others to enjoy.

He loved each one
and grieved their demise;
he considered the chainsaw
the scourge of all creation.

Someday I hope to understand
the spiritual significance
of a shovel
and a bucket of water.

A sapling speaks
as much of hope as a rainbow,
an acorn as deeply as a verse
from the Gospel of John.

Perhaps when I am 90
I will see the truth above my head,
a moment's effort that has become
a beacon in the sky.

Brown-Haired Girl

I see a girl with long brown hair
dancing in a meadow of sunlit wild flowers.

Such delight had been a long time coming.
The days of her childhood are a fading memory.

She left us on a Thursday night
slipping into the snowy sky as soft as a prayer.

I was there and let her go
with a farewell touch and words of encouragement,
"Look to the light." She did
and was gone.

I cannot grieve to see her leave such pain.
She knew the way and took it.

Brown-haired girl with the wavy locks,
dance your freedom in the realm I cannot see.

Give my best to the sun and wind;
fill the meadow with your laughter.

Go where I cannot dance and laugh;
swirl your tresses and touch the hand of God.

I was blessed to be present when my mother died.

Life Is a Gift

"Life is a gift!"
His eyes pierced mine
through the smoke and the noise
of the veterans' hospital hallway.

I remembered the stories he'd told me
of riding his Cayuse pony
to see a farmer's daughter
far out on the Palouse in the early days.

He told of going out for coffee
with his best friend,
then heading for the Dakotas instead,
calling their wives a few days later.

This man lived every day
facing every sunset and sunrise with equal courage.

I could live like that
if I wasn't so concerned
about the score, the balance or the consequences.

To live life as a gift escapes most of us.
We plan and worry, strive and measure,
missing the roses and the smiles,
the sunsets and the snowflakes.

I hope that every once in a while
I find the courage and the wisdom to proclaim,
"Life is a gift!"

Dayton

There is a man
with stories to tell
wisdom to share
most of it true

There is a twinkle
in his eye
knowing that in the telling
there is magic

Crew chief
Farmer
Inventor
Curmudgeon

What-you-see-
is-what-you-get
loveable yet crusty
very Dutch

Such a man leaves
a space
when he is gone

Forgetting him
is not an option

May he rest among the great storytellers
sharing words of wisdom
with a twinkle in his eye
most of it true

Two Men, One Church

Two men
both named John
toil in the tropic sun.
Sweat stains both necks.

One in shirt sleeves
builds a house in Nicaragua.
The other in fatigues
cooks for the U.S. Army in Honduras.

Who would guess they sat together
the week before
in the same church
back in "el norte"?

One holds a trowel,
the other an M-16.
One labors on a wall
soon to have a roof,
his reward
a heartfelt "Gracias!"

The other, startled by the sizzle of a bullet,
returns fire on full-auto,
his reward, the cry, "Got him!"
"Six rounds in the body
from the knees to the head.
Nicaraguan, we think."

When they return to "el norte"
telling their tales
what will their
pastor-brother say?

Turning Forty

"Life's about a week!"
I would not have paid attention
if she had not been
a hundred and five.

Turning forty has a sense
of half-way-ness.
Is my life half over
or am I half way to shore?

An aunt and uncle twice my age
do not help,
celebrating eighty years
of accomplishments
and not much more.

Then there is "Grandy,"
eighty-six and holding fine.
Her body is crippled
but her mind is sharp.
There is passion in this lady
re-reading Kipling long into the night,
longing for her "Ted" and sweet release,
praying to the point of tears
for the next generation.

Yes, I do believe
in the Communion of Saints
and "Life is about a week!"

In the Shadow of a Rose

In the shadow of a rose
I have come to heal my wounds.

I let her fragrance touch
and heal my aching needs.

In the depth of color I find a call
to reach beyond myself.

Roses fade and die,
their fragrance diluted on the breeze.

But the healing and the calling
are carried as a tribute
by all who have rested
and been renewed
in the shadow of a rose.

9

Lessons Learned

Soft Hands

I am being molded,
slowly
carefully
over time.

The hand of God
is shaping me
with surprising
gentleness and patience.

I no longer fear
being crushed by hands
known only
by tradition.

I yield to the process
and the timing.
I am ready
and, for a change, willing.

Paternoster

The years are like
pearls on a string,
each unique
yet identical from a distance.

They gather
one by one,
slowly at first
then more quickly
as if the hands of time
grew nimble with repetition.

I do not fear the end
but yearn to make
each one a blessing
worthy of a memory
and a smile.

Such is the measure
of my eternal wealth,
pearls of great value,
a finished gift to offer
to my Lord
at our meeting.

No Option

Love is no longer
an option.
I cannot love some
and despise others.

Conditional love doesn't work.
It just sits there, like a hunter
waiting for an appropriate
target for its affections.

Love is no longer
an option.
God's call cannot safely
be ignored.

The world is dying
for a few courageous souls
to take off their armor of analysis
and love like there's an endless supply.

Love is no longer
an option.
Either I join the party
or wait outside.

Morning Song

One who rises early
sees things others don't—
the heron, the nuthatch,
the bunny eating breakfast.

My age has robbed me
of long sleep,
compensated for by a nap at mid-day
when my eyelids flutter.

Morning has become my time
for touching the earth,
centering my soul,
embracing the moment.

I do not need a long future
to be present in the here and now,
just to rise with the sun
and be a part of the waking world.

Moment by Moment

I want to see life
with an economy of time
where all the pieces fit
like the incidental clues
of a well-crafted mystery
meaningless at first
then coming together
as essential pieces of a puzzle

I want to live a life
where every moment matters
where nothing is wasted
not a word
not a movement
not a glance
or a gallon of gas

I want a life of conscious intensity
using the moments between heartbeats
to touch off a carefully aimed synapse
that makes a difference at a distance

I don't want much
just all of life
bringing in the energy around me
like an angler reeling in a salmon

Is this too much to ask
of one simple life?

www.ingramcontent.com/pod-product-compliance
Lightning Source LLC
LaVergne TN
LVHW050538100826
845148LV00002B/607